FIRE!

לַהֶסְנֶה אֵינֶנּוּ אֻכָּל

AND THE BUSH WAS
NOT CONSUMED

FIRE!
The Library Is Burning

Barry D. Cytron

Lerner Publications Company • Minneapolis

Library of Congress Cataloging-in-Publication Data

Cytron, Barry D., 1942-
    Fire! : the library is burning.

    Summary: Describes the disastrous 1966 fire at the
library of the Jewish Theological Seminary in New York
City and the massive rescue operation in which both the
neighborhood and the city took part.
    1. Jewish Theological Seminary of America.
Library—History—Juvenile literature. 2. Libraries—
Fires and fire prevention—Juvenile literature.
3. Library materials—Conservation and restoration—
Juvenile literature. 4. Jewish libraries—New York (N.Y.)
—History—Juvenile literature. [1. Jewish Theological
Seminary of America. Library—History. 2. Libraries—
Fire and fire prevention. 3. Library materials—
Conservation and restoration] I. Title.
Z733.J58C9   1988   027.6'3'097471   87-4938
    ISBN 0-8225-0525-8

Manufactured in the United States of America

1   2   3   4   5   6   7   8   9   10   98   97   96   95   94   93   92   91   90   89   88

For Phyllis
and our children
Joseph, Davida, and Naomi

Ian, Kelly, and the children of Riverside Church school

IN THE BEGINNING

It began on April 18, 1966—a beautiful Monday morning in New York City. Ian and Kelly and their classmates Marie Christine and Ichito were laughing and talking as they walked down Broadway to their school at Riverside Church.

Long-legged college students rushed by them. Across the street, classes were beginning at Columbia University. And on the left, other crowds of students made the Barnard College courtyard seem like a blur of color.

Ian, Kelly, Marie Christine, and Ichito hurried on, watching hundreds of dashing bodies race toward classes at still other schools—Teachers College, The Jewish Theological Seminary of America, and Union Theological Seminary. The horns of passing cars honked, and from beneath the sidewalk came the rumbling sound of the subway trains. A busy new week was beginning in their neighborhood.

Soon the children turned the corner. As if to say hello, the voice of a piccolo floated down from the window of yet another school—the Juilliard School of Music. With the high, sweet music in their ears, they skipped up the block to the entrance of Riverside Church.

The kindergarten children had little idea of what went on inside these old, beautiful school buildings. But on this Monday morning, something would happen to change that. The children would discover just how special their neighborhood could be.

THE LIBRARIAN

As Ian and his friends climbed the stairs of Riverside Church, Dr. Menachem Schmelzer walked down Broadway. He was not headed for one of the hundreds of classrooms all around. He was walking toward his office on the fourth floor of the Jewish Theological Seminary of America. True, Dr. Schmelzer was a teacher. He was one of many teachers

Dr. Menachem Schmelzer was in charge of the Seminary library.

8

helping students study to become rabbis and teachers for synagogues throughout the United Sates.

But Dr. Schmelzer did more than teach at the Seminary. He was also the head of the library. Dr. Schmelzer was in charge of the many library workers who took care of the Seminary library. It was an enormous job. Every year thousands of new books and many old and rare books had to be sorted, assigned numbers, and put at the right places on the shelves.

The library was huge. Nearly 250,000 books were neatly lined up on hundreds of metal shelves in the ten floors of the brick Library Tower. And thousands and thousands of magazines and newspapers were stored with them. Nowhere in the world was there a more complete collection of books and magazines about Judaism and being Jewish.

Dr. Schmelzer had much to think about that Monday morning as he made his way to work. But as he climbed the stairs to his office, Dr. Schmelzer had no idea that his job was about to become much more difficult. And he could not imagine that the books he loved and cared for would soon mean so much to Ian and the children of the kindergarten at Riverside Church.

THE FIRST MOMENTS

This beautiful spring morning, a rabbi—one of the professors who taught at the Jewish Theological Seminary school—took a break to look out his office window. Just then, what seemed like a small dark cloud floated skyward. What could it be?

As he watched, he suddenly knew—it was smoke coming from a tiny opening in the library tower. He looked around. Did anyone else see the smoke? Quickly, he picked up his telephone and called the Seminary operator. The operator telephoned the emergency number, calling the Fire Department. At the same moment, a maintenance man named Manuel Garcia thought he smelled smoke coming from somewhere deep among the library shelves. He grabbed a hand-held fire extinguisher and followed the smell into the eighth floor stacks of the Library Tower. Suddenly, the eighth floor was filled with

Fire fighters climbed the ladders to set the water hoses in place.

10

hot flames moving so quickly that, in an instant, the fire was all around him. He hardly knew where to begin putting out such a large fire with such a small extinguisher. Then he saw that the flames were coming from the floor below. Like a dragon, the massive fire was eating its way upward through the library. It puffed out huge, dark clouds of choking smoke as it fed on row after row, and stack after stack, of books and magazines.

With his fire extinguisher empty, Manuel was trapped in a circle of flames. The next thing he knew, he was being pulled out of the smoke. He was very lucky. The fire station was just down the street. The fire trucks and fire fighters were there in a flash. When they heard that someone was on the eighth floor, they bravely rushed into the burning room, found Manuel, and dragged him to safety.

PLANNING THE WATERFALL

The Fire Chief, Alfred Eckert, rushed to the Seminary, too. From below, he saw the thick smoke pouring from the tower and he knew it meant big trouble. He ordered an "all hands" alarm. Soon sirens screamed from every quarter as New York City sent nearly all its hook and ladder trucks, pumpers, and fire fighters to help fight the flames.

Even as the flames were rising, the Fire Chief and the top officers of the Fire Department studied the fire to find the best way to fight it. In the whole Tower, there were just sixteen small windows and one set of stairs. And the fire was spreading upward easily because large sections of the library floors were just open metal grating. That gave the chief an idea, though. He would move the hook and ladder trucks closer to the building and spray water into the tower from the highest openings. Then the water could run down through the open metal floors. That just might halt the spreading flames.

Some fire fighters climbed the long ladders to set the hoses in place. Others put on oxygen masks to protect themselves from the smoke and went into the tower from beneath. Using blankets made of heavy canvas, they covered the scorching, hot metal shelves holding books and magazines that had not yet

The fire fighters took turns resting for a moment.

caught fire. Water would soon cascade like a waterfall down into the lower floors of the library. And, they knew, water can be as dangerous an enemy to books as fire itself. With the shelves covered, they hoped the water would do as little damage as possible.

The fighters were courageous. They were in great danger from the heat and the terrible-smelling green and black smoke. But every moment counted. The books would soon be nothing but ashes unless enough water could be poured in to block the fire's path.

THE SECOND ALARM

Hour after hour passed. The firemen worked from above and from below. The chief worried about the safety of his men. Already, sixty of them had been forced to stop working because they had inhaled too much smoke. And all the fire fighters were growing tired from the difficult work.

At two o'clock that afternoon, Chief Eckert called in a second alarm. Again the sirens blared. Fresh men and equipment were soon working at top speed. Even so, it took three more hours before the Chief declared the fire "under control."

The sun set slowly, and slowly the firemen could see the end in sight. The flames that before were spreading wildly in every direction now only crept along here and there. In a little while, they would be put out forever. For the chief and his troops, the job was about finished.

The fire burned on, and the long day lasted into the night.

WHAT NEXT?

For everyone else at the Seminary, the job was just beginning. The teachers, the students, the office workers, the maintenance people —and especially the library staff—were grateful that no one from the Seminary and none of the fire fighters had been seriously hurt in the fire. At the same time, something very serious and very destructive had happened. The library had nearly burned to the ground.

No one knew on that first day how much had been lost. For the books that had burned, nothing could be done. But what about the thousands of books that had not burned? Just how damaged were they by the water? Could they be rescued?

This story—a true one—is about what happened after the fire. It is a story about the people who helped rescue the books of the Jewish Theological Seminary Library after that terrible day in April 1966. It is a story about the people of New York City and the people of that busy college neighborhood on the Upper West Side.

But it could be a story about any library fire. It could be about the people of any town or city—about any people who love books, build libraries, and read.

EMERGENCY COMMITTEE

That Monday, the raging fire and the thought of what it was doing would not go away. The smell of smoke, the sight of flames, the sounds of sirens and shouting voices haunted every mind. People waited, worried, and spoke quietly to one another. It was Rabbi David Kogen, the man in charge of the day-to-day operation of the Seminary, who finally broke through the silence and the fear, the shock and the pain.

Just as always, he took charge. He began by thinking of people—he wanted to be sure that those who lived and worked in and around the Seminary's buildings would be safe. That evening, while the fire still burned, Rabbi Kogen invited a few very exhausted people to meet with him. Dr. Schmelzer

On the burnt-out eighth floor, everything was destroyed.

was there. So were Jessica Feingold and Carlotta Damanda and Marjorie Wyler.

Usually, Jessica Feingold and Carlotta Damanda spent their time inviting ministers and priests from New York City's many churches to study at the Seminary. From her office, Mrs. Wyler sent information about the school to newspapers, magazines, and radio and television stations. Together these three women kept the Seminary in touch with the neighborhood and the world.

The group spent hours thinking together. Should classes be canceled? Could they find rooms for the many students who lived at the Seminary? There were many other questions. At midnight, as the five people got ready to go home, they heard the first good news of the day—the fire was out.

The good news brought with it a thousand new questions. Had any books survived the flames? Could they be salvaged? Had this ever happened to a library before? Who could tell them what to do?

There were no easy answers to their questions. Some answers would have to wait until they had the report of the Fire Chief. But the fire had just been extinguished, and it was too soon for the Chief to report. Right now, it was very late. As the five co-workers said good night, walked through the courtyard, and headed home at last, they knew one thing for sure—the next day would be even harder.

SEEING THE DESTRUCTION

Tuesday morning, Fire Chief Eckert met with the emergency committee. "Everything is looking all right in the Tower," he told them. "The clean-up can start soon. Right now, Dr. Schmelzer can join my men and me. We're going to walk through the library stacks to see the damage."

Dr. Schmelzer put on a heavy rubber fireman's coat and thick fire galoshes—strange clothing for a head librarian. Following the Fire Chief, he climbed the stairs into the stacks. Since the moment the fire began, he had

Pages of books were scattered everywhere.

tried to imagine what his library would look like afterward. All his imaginings had been like a nightmare. What he saw was even worse.

Using flashlights, Dr. Schmelzer and the fire fighters peered through blackened stacks at what had been the eighth floor of the library. They were standing in sludge that came to the top of their boots. Everywhere they stepped, their feet crushed the soggy remains of charred books and bits of magazines. And where the books had stood—all the librarian could see by the firemen's beacon were shelves, thick with ashes. No books. No pages. Just ashes. Ashes. Everywhere.

THE FIRE AND THE WATER

Silently, with the firemen to guide him, Dr. Schmelzer climbed the narrow steps to the ninth floor and finally the top. It was all alike. It was gone.

On the way down, they stopped at the seventh floor. Dr. Schmelzer expected to see more of the same. But here he could see the outlines of books. Some were burned entirely. Others stood swollen, bursting with water. Some were in place on the shelf, looking just as they had the morning the fire began. But they were so heavy with water that the shelves they were on were twisted into strange forms.

Many books on this floor were were wet through and through. They were so soaked that as Dr. Schmelzer lifted them from the shelf, water poured out. Others were just moist to the touch, like sponges recently used. But none had escaped being hit by at least some of the thousands of gallons of water that had been pumped in to put out the flames.

As Dr. Schmelzer and the fire fighters wound their way downstairs to the lower levels, things began to look better. The further down they moved from the eighth floor where the fire had started, the better shape the books were in. Dr. Schmelzer could not be certain because it was such a quick walk-through, but he thought that about two-thirds of the books were still in fairly good condition. It was just possible they could be saved.

Hand to hand, the books were passed along.

After hurrying back to the emergency committee, Dr. Schmelzer spoke to them of what he had seen.

"We must not lose hope," he said gently. "But we must act quickly to remove the books. They are filled with water and if they are left in the tower too long, they will soon become moldy. We need a plan to empty the stacks, and we need some way to dry the covers and the pages." The group in Rabbi Kogen's office decided to call for all the Seminary's students and teachers and any volunteers to be on hand the next morning.

THE HUMAN CHAIN

Early Wednesday morning, the neighborhood was transformed. It seemed as if everyone was ready to lend a hand. Librarians from the nearby colleges offered to loan their library wagons and book carts. The sidewalks rumbled as carts were wheeled down the street. A moving company, Neptune Van Lines, hearing the report of the fire, sent their trucks to deliver thousands of boxes in which to move the books. Upper Broadway began to look more like a factory center than a college neighborhood.

Most important of all were the volunteers. Students, from the Seminary and Columbia, from across the street and across town, rushed to help. Teachers and rabbis stood in line with their pupils. And folks from the neighborhood who cared about schools and books were there, too. Hardly a suit or tie was to be seen. Everyone came in old clothes, ready to work.

Gathering everyone together, Dr. Schmelzer and his co-workers formed the volunteers into human chains stretching for hundreds of feet. One person beside another, the chains wound upward into the dark chambers of the burned out Tower. With no tools but their hands and no task but to lift, the work began.

What they did was simple. The first person in each chain took a pile of books off the shelf, let the water gush out, and then passed the books back to the second person, who passed the stack of books to the third person—from one pair of hands to the next waiting pair of hands. Eager, caring hands

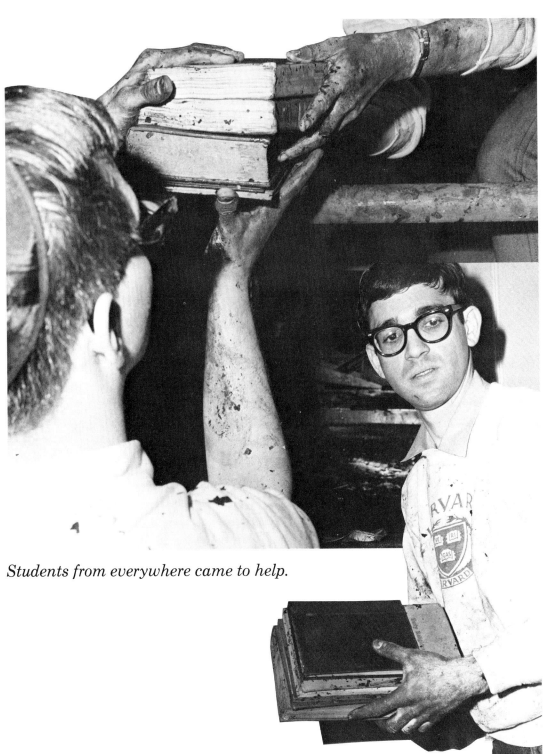

Students from everywhere came to help.

passed books from the blackened upper floors of the Tower down the winding metal stairs.

It was a human conveyor belt. First a few—then massive numbers of books—emerged from the shadows of the foul-smelling library. At the bottom end of the lines, more volunteers packed the stacks of drenched volumes into boxes, loaded the boxes onto carts, and wheeled the carts out of the building.

APARTMENTS OF BOOKS

A t first, the volunteers tried to keep the books in order as they were taken out. After all, a library is more than just books on shelves—each book is in a certain place on a certain shelf so it can be found when needed. So the volunteers tried to keep books coming off the same shelf together. This made the work go slower. "Should we give up, and just pack books in any box?" the volunteers asked Dr. Schmelzer.

The librarian thought for a few minutes. He knew how much work it takes to keep books in their right places and keep shelves in order. But right now, time was the great enemy. It was most important to work as quickly as possible. Finally, he told the volunteers: "For now, we'll have to forget about the order. Let's just get the books out!"

At the end of the human chains, cartons of soaked books were being piled higher and higher. Where would they go?

Luckily, one of the Seminary people found a place to store the books—just a short walk up the street. Next door to the Seminary were two large, old apartment buildings owned by the school. When these buildings were bought, the Seminary planned to tear them down and, in their place, to construct a new library. But there never seemed to be enough money for the project, and, in the end, the apartments sat there empty, waiting.

Because the buildings were old and rickety, the Seminary people had to check with the city government to be sure that it was all right to store the books there. As soon as the city gave its permission, the workers began wheeling cart after cart of books up the block. The apartments were unlocked,

Pulling the books, boxing them up, and carting them up the street

24

the floors were swept clean, and the boxes were carried one at a time up the stairs.

Inside the two buildings, students emptied the boxes on the apartment floors. Carefully, they opened the books and stood them on end. By standing the volumes upright, they hoped, some of the water might evaporate from the pages. It was not the best way to dry the books, but it was surely better than leaving them in the boxes.

One after the other, the apartments filled with books. There were books on the floors, in the cabinets, atop every counter, even in the sinks! Any place that could hold an open book did.

MOLD

For days and days, this process continued. Pull the books. Pass them down. Box them up. Move them to carts. Cart them to the apartments. Uncrate them. Open them up. Stand them up. It was slow and tiring and tedious. Every morning the volunteers came to work, and every evening they went home, exhausted. But the books were being rescued.

One day, the children from the kindergarten at Riverside Church stopped by on their way home from school. They were curious. "What's going on?" they asked. "Why are you packing all those books in boxes? And where are you taking all those boxes? And why is everybody in such a rush?"

A Seminary librarian who was walking by answered the children. "If you want, I'll show you. You see," she said to them as she took one book from a box, "when water gets into a book, this is what happens. The water turns any dust in the book into a thin film of mud. And the bindings of the books, made from colored leather, begin to bleed. Then the color from the leather smears the pages.

"Worse than that, the water begins to dissolve chemicals in the paper. As the chemicals melt, the bacteria which are always in the air feast on this 'meal'; first the pages turn slimy, then green, and then brown. That's called

Rabbi David Kogen worried that the books—standing open in the apartments—were not drying fast enough.

mold. Mold doesn't care how old or rare or wonderful books may be. The mold just keeps 'eating away' at the books until it destroys them entirely."

The librarian led the children into one apartment. She showed them how the books were set on end to dry. Ian, Kelly, Marie Christine, Ichito, and their friends watched the students work, and asked many questions. By then, it was getting late, so the librarian took them to the door, where everyone said goodbye.

AN OLD, NEW IDEA

In the apartment houses, the books were drying a little at a time. But after a few days, it was clear that only the pages directly exposed to the air were drying. And, because the books had to sit open and on end, the open pages were beginning to wrinkle. Even if the books really did dry this way, they would end up misshapen, and they might be impossible to read anyway.

More and more Rabbi Kogen recalled a memory from his youth. In Europe, where he was born, Jews prepared for the Spring holiday of Passover in many ways. One way was by cleaning house—even cleaning books! He remembered how people used to take their books outside and spread them open on the lawn to air. Dust and crumbs which had fallen between the pages while the books were being used, were carried away by the gentle breeze flapping through the fluttering pages.

"What if we took some of our books and spread them out in the courtyard?" suggested Rabbi Kogen. "Wouldn't that help dry them?" No sooner had he spoken than the job began. By afternoon, volunteers were spreading books out in long rows. And it worked. With the help of sun and fresh air, the pages of the books dried—most of them in two or three days.

But there were two problems. First, there was nowhere near enough room for all the books. There were almost one hundred and eighty thousand volumes to dry and only a few hundred feet of lawn space. If the job were done this way, it would take years to complete. In the meantime, thousands of

Volunteer helpers carefully placed the books out in the open air.

books would be destroyed by mold.

Second, drying books in the open air was only good when the sun was shining. But it was springtime in New York, and it often rained.

Even though Rabbi Kogen's fresh air idea did not work to save all the books, it did another very important thing: It reminded the people on the emergency committee that not all the books saved from the stacks were equally important. Thinking about that, the staff people knew they had to make decisions about which books were most important and which should be dried out first.

A SPECIAL KIND OF LIBRARY

I n one way, the Jewish Theological Seminary library is different from public and school libraries. Most libraries collect modern books—written in the last fifty years. Most of these books are in English. And public and school libraries collect books on all kinds of things—from dancing to computers to sports.

But the Seminary library collects only books and magazines needed by the people who come to study at the Seminary. It is a special collection for students preparing to serve as teachers and rabbis and for scholars who study the Jewish people. The 250,000 books owned by the Seminary were texts in Bible and religious thought and magazines and pamphlets about Jewish history and the Jewish way of life.

The books of the Seminary were in dozens of different languages. Not only English, but Hebrew, Yiddish, and Ladino—languages Jews used in prayer and daily life for the last two thousand years—and works in ancient tongues not spoken in more than two thousand years—like Syriac, Aramaic, and ancient Greek. And there were many books written in the languages of countries where Jews have lived—books in Polish, Russian, Spanish, and French.

Many of the books in the Seminary library were printed hundreds of years ago. Many were one of a kind. The Emergency Committee was most worried

Blessed by the spring sun, some books did dry.

about these valuable, older, and rare volumes. While they loved all books and believed that all were important, they knew that certain books could never be replaced. These had to be saved first, if it was at all possible.

THE SEARCH

The committee asked teachers and librarians to find these books among all the books in all the apartments. While many volunteers continued pulling books from the burned out library, others began to sort the books that had already been removed. The librarians and professors—and even some of the more learned students—pitched in. They picked up each book again. They studied the title page to see when the book was published, who the author was, and what the book was about.

Was it a book about astronomy written in sixteenth-century Holland? Was it a medical text written in Hebrew when Jews still lived in Spain? Or was it a manual for observance of Jewish customs, written in Arabic somewhere in North Africa? The books were dirty, the pages were hard to read, and the work was not very pleasant. It took a great many days to sift through the books again, to pick out the most precious ones.

A NEW KIND OF VOLUNTEER

Rabbi Kogen knew that they were losing the battle against time. Some books were drying. But the spring rains stole too much sunshine. And time was passing too quickly. No matter how many books they took outside to air and no matter how many times they turned the books in the apartments, most of the books were showing hints of that sickening green mold.

The most surprising telephone call came from the headquarters of General Foods.

What they needed was a new idea—something to give the Emergency Committee and the volunteers new hope. When it came, it was a real surprise.

In the morning, the phone rang in Mrs. Wyler's office. "Can I help you?" Mrs. Wyler asked. The man on the other end began to speak.

"You don't know me," the man said, "but I read about your fire in *The New York Times* newspaper. I think we can help save the books."

At first, Mrs. Wyler thought that the man wanted to volunteer. So many people called every day to offer their help, and, of course, every call was a welcome one, and every helper was a strong pair of hands and a warm heart to rely on. But this time it was different. This man was not just offering his own help. He was calling to offer the help of one of the largest companies in the United States.

The company was General Foods, a name known far and wide. General Foods makes *Post Grape Nuts* cereal, *Log Cabin* syrup, *Jello* gelatin dessert, *Maxwell House* coffee, and many other name brands of foods and coffee. The man was an officer of General Foods, and his new idea came from a new kind of coffee!

FREEZE AND DRY THEM

That year, 1966, General Foods pioneered a new way to make instant coffee. The old way—used by nearly all coffee companies—was to spray-dry coffee into tiny grains that could be used with hot water to make fresh coffee at home. The new way was totally new. First, the company brewed real coffee, just as we do at home. Then they froze the hot liquid. Once frozen, they used special ovens to extract—to pull out—all the water from the frozen coffee. They called their new kind of coffee "freeze-dried."

The officer from General Foods thought that the freeze-drying idea might work for the soaked books, just as it did for coffee. After explaining, he said, "What if we send some of our test ovens and some of our food scientists who know how to use them to your school? What do you think?"

Dr. Zucker, a Seminary professor, searched for the most valuable books to freeze-dry in the test ovens.

Mrs. Wyler was excited. "Absolutely! Let's try it! Right away!" Dr. Schmelzer and Rabbi Kogen were delighted. This could be the idea they had been hoping for. They called electricians to "pull" in the large electrical power lines needed to give energy to the big ovens.

The food scientists from General Foods arrived the next morning to begin experimenting. The library staff selected some of the most precious of the water-logged books. "Let's start with these," they said.

One by one, the scientists weighed each book to find how much water was in it. They set the ovens to extract just exactly that amount of water. Then they placed the books in the oven, and turned the power on. In a flash, the machines were finished. Almost like magic, the ovens seemed to lift the water out from the pages and away from the binding. Book after book, one by one, the scientists put a wet mess into the oven, and seconds later, they had a perfectly dry, absolutely normal-looking book.

Everyone rejoiced. Finally there was a way to dry all the books that had been lugged to safety. But their happiness soon ended. The ovens were speedy, but before they could be turned on, the scientists had to weigh and measure each book and decide how much extra water was in it. The ovens took no time; figuring out how to use them took too much time.

In the end, the idea from the people at General Foods was a little like the Rabbi Kogen's fresh air idea. It worked well, but it was slow—and, for the books, time was running out. The rejoicing turned to disappointment. The volunteers and the staff began to lose heart again. They needed a faster way to dry the books—and soon.

THE GIFT

J ust then, a student named Bayla Bonder brought a gift to Rabbi Kogen—one of the books from the apartments. A very special one. One that had not been dried by the sun, and had not been dried by the ovens. Yet it was dry and free of mold. What was the secret? How was it done? When Bayla explained her idea, it seemed too simple to be true.

They dried the books page by page . . .

Before she brought the idea to Rabbi Kogen, Bayla tested it on her own. She took paper towels from a restroom and placed them between the pages of the book. As the towels filled with water, she took them out and put in new, dry towels. Before long, the book was dry!

Rabbi Kogen liked the idea. It was not as exciting as freeze-drying books, but it looked like it might really work. Right away, library staff people tried Bayla's plan on a few more books. They were amazed. The soft paper towels embraced the pages; the pages willingly gave up water.

Dr. Schmelzer met with the Emergency Committee again the next day. "I feel sure this is our best chance. But we are talking about thousands of books. Where will we get enough hands and enough towels?"

Once again, Rabbi Kogen turned to Mrs. Wyler and Ms. Damanda. With hope in his voice, he spoke to them: "We've asked people to do so much in these last seven days. Do you think they have the energy left to help us some more?" The women agreed among themselves: "No doubt about it, Rabbi. People want to help. We think they will be thrilled to hear that this idea works so well. We'll get the word out!"

WITH HANDS AND TOWELS

The work began anew. Ms. Damanda spent days finding and buying enough paper towels. She called every paper merchant she could find. Paper towels came from everywhere. Mrs. Wyler sent announcements to newspapers, magazines, radio, and television. And people came from everywhere.

Some private schools gave their students time off to help. College students and university teachers and workers pitched in once more, as they had when they made the human chains to take the books from the Library Tower. And many, many other New Yorkers—those who lived in the neighborhood or who heard of the fire on the radio or read about it in their newspaper—came to share their time and their strength. Now there were enough hands to do the job.

. . . book by book—they used only their hands and paper towels.

INTERLEAFING

Anew word was born. The volunteers called their work "interleafing." And they were doing just that—opening leaf after leaf of nearly one hundred and eighty thousand books, slipping in dry towels, watching to see when the towels were filled with water, and doing this a second and even a third time—as long as it took to dry each and every book.

And it took many weeks and thousands of hands—hands of Jews and Christians; the young, the middle-aged, and the elderly; students studying to read Hebrew and those studying to read music; business people and scholars. The tables and chairs in the main room of the library were always full. The library seemed more like a picnic park. Among the piles of boxes, mounds of towels, and heaps of books sat volunteers, working and talking together like old friends—though they had met that day or the day before.

The people of the Jewish Theological Seminary wanted very much to thank these wonderful helpers. One way they tried to do this was by keeping the cafeteria open day and night, handing out free meals and snacks to everyone. Of course, this was only a small way of thanking them.

Everyone—Seminary people and the volunteers—knew that the real thanks was the work itself. The volunteers were being rewarded in a special way. For the rescue effort gave the workers the only chance they might ever have to save not just a library but a civilization.

The Seminary library—like libraries everywhere—is filled with ideas, memories, and hopes. We love libraries and books for that reason. In libraries we find answers to questions people have asked throughout the ages—why we fall in love, why we fight, how we seek peace, how we build, what we believe, why we work.

The Seminary library is just such a collection of answers—a special record of the Jewish people, ever changing and growing. And the people who came to "interleaf" were helping to rescue the long written record of that civilization.

The kindergarten class of Riverside Church planned a cookie sale.

IMPORTANT HELPERS

While many kinds of people helped the library rescue its books, one group was very special. These were the children from the kindergarten class at Riverside Church—Ian, Kelly, Marie Christine, Ichito, and their classmates—the same ones who heard the fire engines roar the first day of the disaster and who watched the clean-up every day as they passed the Seminary.

For a long while, the children in the Church School searched to find a way to help. Finally, they decided to bake cookies, sell them in the neighborhood, and give the money to the library. With their teachers' help, the youngsters spent a whole week on their project—making the cookie batter, baking the cookies in the Church kitchen, hand-wrapping the cookies, and lovingly tying a decoration around each one.

Then they set up a little stand near the Seminary school building, where they sold their goodies to passers-by. Imagine how excited they were as people came to buy. In just a few hours, they sold every cookie, and raised sixty-two dollars and sixty-five cents! To Ian and Kelly and the others, it seemed like a fortune, indeed.

THE CHANCELLOR

The next morning, the kindergarten class walked to the Seminary to deliver the money they raised to Chancellor Louis Finkelstein, the professor and scholar who was the head of the Jewish Theological Seminary. Along with the money, they gave him this note:

Dear Doctor Finkelstein:

We are kindergarten children at Riverside Church in Room 615. We wanted to earn some money to help you replace your books. We thought of selling cookies. We baked cookies for four days. We baked about 500 cookies. We sold them for five cents each. We loved doing it. We are sorry the books got burned. Love, . . .

The Riverside Church children brought their gift to Chancellor Louis Finkelstein.

And the note was signed with the printed names of all twenty-five children from the Church class. Dr. Finkelstein was especially pleased by the children's note and the work they had done, too. Later, he wrote to them. In his letter, he thanked them for being so kind and working so hard. He told them that their cookie sale was one of many generous acts done by the Seminary's friends and neighbors.

"At a time of deep sadness," Dr. Finkelstein wrote, "this knowledge that so many people shared our loss and wanted to help has brought us great comfort."

When Doctor Finkelstein wrote that he felt "deep sadness," that was because, of all the people who taught and worked at the Seminary, he had been there the longest. As Chancellor of the school, he was well known throughout the country. A kind and wise man, he had seen the school grow rich in students and teachers. He also had watched the library blossom into the largest Jewish collection in the world. For him, maybe more than for almost anyone else around the school, the library fire was truly a "deep sadness."

ONE LAST TASK

One day, several months after the fire, Dr. Finkelstein asked Rabbi Kogen into his office.

"David," the Chancellor said, "one important task remains from the fire. Will you help?" "Of course," Rabbi Kogen answered. "What do we need to do?"

"David," Dr. Finkelstein said, "The time has come to bury the Danzig *Torahs*. And one more thing," the Chancellor added. "I want to be there when it's done."

Rabbi Kogen knew about the Danzig *Torahs*, and knew, too, that something had to be done about them. The terrible sorrow in Dr. Finkelstein's voice and the suddenness with which the Chancellor asked him to help

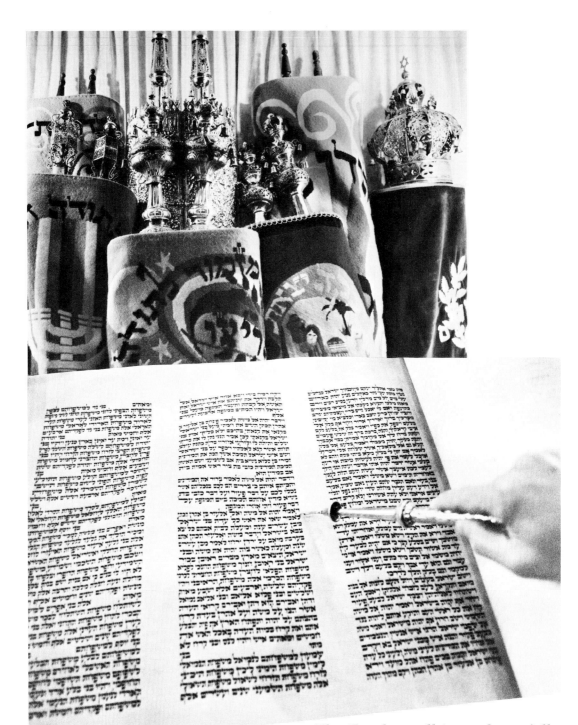

The Torah scroll is read carefully, using a pointer to mark the place.

44

saddened Rabbi Kogen, too.

Rabbi Kogen knew that these *Torah* scrolls were the most precious things destroyed in the fire. He also knew that the scrolls to be buried were doubly special because of their history.

SCROLLS OF HOLINESS

Since early times, *Torah* scrolls—long parchment rolls—have been written by hand in beautifully formed Hebrew script. They contain the first five books of the Bible, the Books of Moses. The scrolls are the most sacred possessions of the Jewish people. They are handled with care and tenderness. When they are studied during Jewish prayer services, they are gently placed on a desk, where members of the congregation read out loud from them, using a pointer shaped like a hand to keep their place in the text. In that way, the readers are sure not to smear the special ink or mar the parchment by touching the Hebrew writing with their own hands.

When a *Torah* scroll is damaged in any way or wears out after years of use, the Jewish custom is to bury it. In that way, the *Torah* is given the same honor given to the body of a person who has died. Most Jewish cemeteries have a plot of land set aside in which to bury sacred scrolls and other holy books which are no longer usable. Rabbi Kogen called a cemetery near New York City and made all the plans for the burial. For the holy scrolls, this seemed normal enough, but there was more to know.

SCROLLS OF DANZIG

The *Torah* scrolls that Dr. Finkelstein wanted to bury were special because all *Torah* scrolls are. And for another reason, too. These forty scrolls burned in the Seminary fire came from a small city beside the Baltic Sea in northern Europe. Today, that town is part of Poland, and its

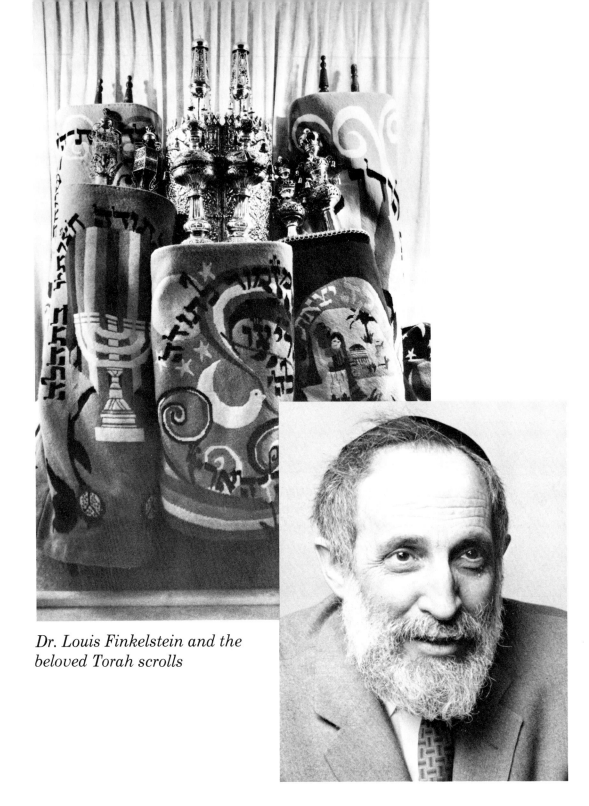

Dr. Louis Finkelstein and the beloved Torah scrolls

name is Gdansk.

In 1938, the city was known by its German name, Danzig. In that year, the city's Jewish population, nearly 10,000 women, men and children, were frightened. The year before, there were attacks against the Jewish community by the German Nazis. Two synagogues were destroyed, many people had suffered, and now the leaders feared that more rioting was coming. They believed there was great danger ahead for the Jews of Danzig.

After much thinking and talking, the Jewish leaders asked everyone—from the infants to the elderly and all in between—to leave. They hoped the Jews of Danzig might find new homes in a new land, a land that would welcome them, a land that would protect them from the evils of Nazi Germany and its leader, Adolf Hitler. It took many months to make plans for so many people, but the leaders knew they were doing the right thing.

SCROLLS OF REMEMBRANCE

O nce the leaders believed their people would be safe, they had to decide what to do with the many ancient treasures that belonged to the whole community. These were the official documents and books and synagogue ritual objects used and collected by the Jewish residents of Danzig through hundreds of years.

The search for a safe place—away from the war in Europe—to send these priceless things led to Dr. Finkelstein and the Jewish Theological Seminary of America. Dr. Finkelstein offered to care for anything the Danzig leaders sent. In 1939, crate upon crate arrived in New York, carrying the precious synagogue decorations and objects and books. The *Torah* scrolls were in these crates.

The Jews of Danzig never returned to their homes. After the war, most of the treasures were placed in the Jewish Museum, a part of the Seminary that has its own building in a different part of New York City. There, the treasures can be seen and shared by visitors from every corner of the world.

*The sacred scrolls were buried
in the cemetery.*

The *Torah* scrolls, however, did not belong in a museum. They were treasures of a different kind—scrolls of remembrance—and Dr. Finkelstein watched as they were carefully packed and placed on the tenth floor of the Library Tower for safekeeping.

Now, many years later, everything on the tenth floor was destroyed by the fire. All that remained from the *Torahs* given over to Dr. Finkelstein's care were charred scrolls, scraps, and ashes. This is what the Seminary people buried in that New York cemetery.

THE WAY BACK

After the burial was over, Dr. Finkelstein, Rabbi Kogen, and Dr. Schmelzer drove away from the cemetery together. They talked, but, try as they might, Rabbi Kogen and Dr. Schmelzer could find no words to help Dr. Finkelstein overcome his sadness.

As the car neared the Seminary, Rabbi Kogen caught sight of the Library Tower. Just a few months ago, that ten-story building was spilling out mountains of smoke. Now it stood silent. The black smoke stains around the windows were the only reminder of what happened. On this day, however, Rabbi Kogen looked not at the black stains, but at the sculpture in the middle of the Tower.

There, in simple white stone was the emblem of the Jewish Theological Seminary—a Burning Bush with three Hebrew words. The Torah tells how Moses was walking in the wilderness when he turned aside at the sight of a bush burning on a mountainside. As Moses came closer, he saw that, despite the flames, the bush was not turning to ashes. It was burning, and yet it remained alive and strong.

The Bible tells us that, at that spot, Moses heard God command him to go and rescue his people from slavery in Egypt. Ever since, the Burning Bush has been a holy symbol to the Jewish people. It reminds us that a lowly thorn bush can be as sacred as a great mountain and that learning may be found anywhere we turn aside to look carefully. It also teaches us how important it

AND THE BUSH WAS
NOT CONSUMED

is to care for others, as Moses was told to care for the slaves.

Soon after the Seminary was founded, the Burning Bush was chosen as the school's symbol. The artist who designed the sculpture for the Library Tower carved the Bush in flames. Underneath he placed the Hebrew words from the Bible that tell of Moses' vision: "And the Bush was not consumed."

From the automobile, Rabbi Kogen pointed to the Burning Bush on the Library Tower. How wise the Seminary founders were to choose that emblem, he said to Dr. Finkelstein and Dr. Schmelzer. For the lessons of the Burning Bush lived on in all the volunteers had done those months following the fire. Their actions—lifting books, passing them down the human chains, carting them to safety, carrying them up the apartment house stairs, standing them up on end, "freeze-drying," inspecting, and "interleafing" them—were all great lessons in caring and sharing.

The spirit of the Burning Bush still lived. Though the great library had burned in flames, it, like the Burning Bush, could not be destroyed.

It was true that Rabbi Kogen and Dr. Finkelstein and Dr. Schmelzer had just returned from burying sacred *Torahs* which could not be saved. But they had also witnessed a great event—as people of many religions, ages, skin colors, and beliefs joined hands one tragic and beautiful spring—to save the books of the Seminary library so that people everywhere could read and study forever the living lessons of the past.

For 17 years, this pre-fab building was used for restoring and housing the books that had been rescued from the fire.

The beautiful new Seminary library was dedicated on December 4, 1983.

THE STORY GOES ON

Returning the library to a usable condition took not just months but many years. Once the books were completely dried out, they were examined to determine if they had to be rebound. Then the librarians wrote a special combination of letters and numbers on the spine of each book. This method of labeling books is called Library of Congress cataloging, and it was done so the books could be arranged in an orderly, easy-to-find way on the shelves.

This work required thousands of hours of labor and millions of dollars. To do the job adequately, a large, temporary pre-fab building was constructed in the school's courtyard. Here the librarians would finally determine the extent of the fire's damage to the books—that the flames and water had completely destroyed 85,000 volumes. It was also inside this temporary building that the library staff set about restoring every one of the remaining 165,000 books.

While the librarians continued their work, the Seminary leaders had to decide what to do with all of the restored books as well as the new ones that were being purchased. Should the burned-out Tower be remodeled or should a new building be constructed? After much discussion, everyone agreed that it was time to construct a new building.

More years passed while the necessary money was raised from thousands of people. Finally, in 1980, construction crews with their tools and cranes arrived at the Seminary campus to begin the project. In the autumn of 1983, 17 years after the terrible flames had done their damage, a ribbon-cutting ceremony was held, and the doors to a beautiful, large, modern building were opened.

This multi-story building had a spacious area for storing the vast collection of books and magazines. There were also special rooms where students and teachers could consult the latest materials on Jewish thought and religion. And there were even computers and TVs.

Because Judaism is a very ancient religion, students of Judaica often need to consult not only recent books but also those printed years ago. When students happen to take one of the older books from a shelf, they will often notice that the book looks different from the newer ones. Its pages may be a bit warped, or its binding may not be as smooth or as neat as that of a newer book. Perhaps those wrinkles will remind students that the book they are holding was once saved from a terrible fire. They may even recall the story of how many caring people rescued that book and thousands and thousands of other books just as precious. And, perhaps, as they hold that book in their hands, they will feel the "binding" of the past to the future with each new generation of students who comes to learn and to grow.

ABOUT THE AUTHOR

Barry D. Cytron is the rabbi of Adath Jeshurun Congregation, a large Conservative synagogue in Minneapolis. He moved to his present home from Des Moines, Iowa in 1983, where he was the rabbi for eleven years at Tifereth Israel Synagogue.

Rabbi Cytron was born in St. Louis, Missouri, and went to college at Columbia University in New York City. He was ordained as a rabbi at the Jewish Theological Seminary of America. During his second year in the Seminary, the fire about which he writes nearly destroyed the famous library. With hundreds of other people, he worked to rescue the books.

The idea for the book came to him after he told the story one day to the women of the Des Moines congregation. His wife, Phyllis, improved the story in many ways, and his children have always been ready to listen to yet another version of it. The people of the Seminary were very cooperative, and friends in Minneapolis were willing to help him locate all the photographs which are part of the book.

Rabbi Cytron enjoys running, listening to classical music, and now that he has a computer at his desk, writing. In 1986, he and his friend Earl Schwartz wrote *When Life Is in the Balance*, which examines the Jewish teachings on life and death issues.

PHOTO ACKNOWLEDGEMENTS

Front Cover	Courtesy of The Jewish Theological Seminary of America (J.T.S.A.)
Back Cover	Courtesy of J.T.S.A./photo by Arnold Katz
Page 6	Courtesy of The Riverside Church/photo by Cash Baxter
Page 8	Courtesy of J.T.S.A./(top) photo by John Popper
Page 10	Photo by John Olson
Page 12	Photo by John Olson
Page 14 Left	Photo by John Olson
Page 14 Right	(Both) Courtesy of J.T.S.A.
Page 16	Coutesy of J.T.S.A./photo by Arnold Katz
Page 18	Courtesy of J.T.S.A./photo by Arnold Katz
Page 20	Courtesy of J.T.S.A./photo by Arnold Katz
Page 22	Courtesy of J.T.S.A./photos by Arnold Katz
Page 24	Courtesy of J.T.S.A./(left) photo by Arnold Katz, (right) photo by Benno Schapira
Page 26	Courtesy of J.T.S.A./(bottom) photo by Arnold Katz, (top) photo by John Popper
Page 28	Courtesy of J.T.S.A./photos by Arnold Katz
Page 30	Courtesy of J.T.S.A./photo by Arnold Katz
Page 32	Courtesy of General Foods Corporation
Page 34 Left	Courtesy of J.T.S.A./photo by Benno Schapira
Page 34 Right	Courtesy of General Foods Corporation
Page 36	Courtesy of J.T.S.A./(left) photo by Arnold Katz, (right) photo by Benno Schapira
Page 38	Courtesy of J.T.S.A./photos by Arnold Katz
Page 40	Courtesy of The Riverside Church/photo by Bill Anderson
Page 42 Top	Courtesy of J.T.S.A.
Page 42 Bottom	Courtesy of The Riverside Church
Page 44	Photos by William Rosenfeld
Page 46 Top	Photo by William Rosenfeld
Page 46 Bottom	Courtesy of J.T.S.A.
Page 48	Photos by William Rosenfeld
Page 50	Courtesy of J.T.S.A.
Page 52	Courtesy of J.T.S.A./photos by John Popper